Alfred's

Music for Little Mozarts

Written Activities and Rhythm Pat...
to Reinforce Rhythm Reading

The *Rhythm Speller Book 2* reinforces rhythm skills based on the concepts introduced in the *Music Lesson Book 2*. The pages in the book correlate page by page with the materials in the *Music Lesson Book*. They should be assigned according to the instructions in the upper right corner of the pages in this book. They may also be assigned as review material at any time after the students have passed the designated *Music Lesson Book* page.

Each page of the *Rhythm Speller Book* has two activities—a **rhythm-writing** activity and a **rhythm-reading** activity. The written activities reinforce note values and counting through coloring, circling, drawing, or matching. The rhythm-reading activities help students practice:

• Clapping or tapping rhythm patterns while counting aloud.

• Playing rhythms on rhythm instruments or keys on the keyboard. (Other rhythm instruments can be substituted for those suggested throughout the book.)

• Chanting words based on rhythm patterns.

Alfred Music
P.O. Box 10003
Van Nuys, CA 91410-0003
alfred.com

ISBN-10: 1-4706-4051-1
ISBN-13: 978-1-4706-4051-4

Illustrations by Christine Finn

Christine H. Barden · Gayle Kowalchyk · E. L. Lancaster

Rhythm Writing

Circle each **dotted half note** with a **green** crayon.

Draw an **X** through each **half note** and **quarter note**.

A Dotted Half Note gets 3 counts.

Count: 1 - 2 - 3

Rhythm Reading

1 Tap the rhythm pattern on your lap. Count aloud.

Tap:

Count: 1   1   1   1 - 2 - 3   1 - 2 - 3   1 - 2 - 3

2 Play the above rhythm pattern with a tambourine.

Rhythm Writing

Draw a line connecting the dots to match the rhythm patterns to their counts.

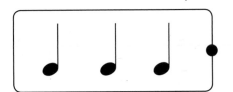

1 - 2   1 - 2

1   1   1

1 - 2 - 3

Rhythm Reading

Clap the *Clara Schumann-Cat* rhythm pattern and chant the words.

Clap:

Chant: **Cla   -   ra   Schu - mann - Cat   (rest)**

Use with page 11.

Rhythm Writing

1 Circle the notes that get 1 count with a **brown** crayon.

2 Circle the notes that get 2 counts with a **blue** crayon.

3 Circle the notes that get 3 counts with a **yellow** crayon.

4 Circle the notes that get 4 counts with a **green** crayon.

Rhythm Reading

1 Clap and count the rhythm pattern.

Clap:

Count: 1   1   1   1   1   1   1   rest

2 Using finger 4 of the RH, play the above rhythm pattern on any F. Then, play again with RH finger 2.

Rhythm Writing

Change each **whole note** to a **dotted half note** by:

1. Tracing it.

2. Drawing a stem going up on the right.

3. Adding a dot on the right.

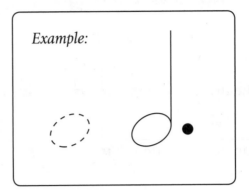

Example:

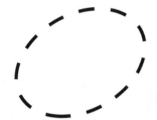 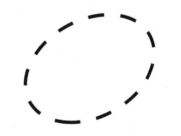 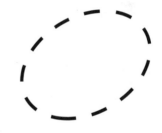

Rhythm Reading

1. Clap and count the rhythm pattern.

Clap:

Count: 1 - 2 - 3   1 - 2 - 3   1   1   1   1 - 2 - 3

2. Play the above rhythm pattern on a triangle.

Use with page 15.

Rhythm Writing

1 Circle the rhythm pattern 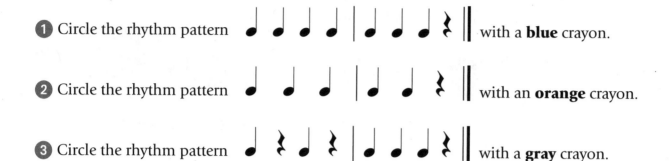 with a **blue** crayon.

2 Circle the rhythm pattern  with an **orange** crayon.

3 Circle the rhythm pattern  with a **gray** crayon.

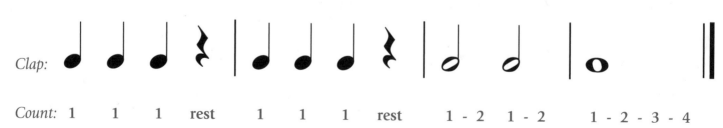

Rhythm Reading

1 Clap and count the rhythm pattern.

Clap:

Count: 1   1   1   rest   1   1   1   rest   1 - 2   1 - 2   1 - 2 - 3 - 4

2 Using finger 2 of the RH, play the above rhythm pattern on any G.
Then, play again with RH finger 3.

Rhythm Writing

Draw a line connecting the dots to match the rhythm patterns to their counts.

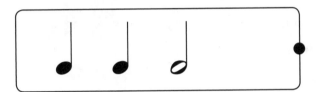

Rhythm Reading

Clap and count the rhythm patterns.

1

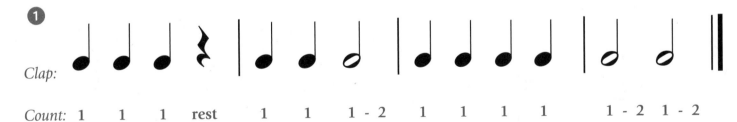

Clap:

Count: 1   1   1   rest   1   1   1 - 2   1   1   1   1   1 - 2 1 - 2

2

Clap:

Count: 1   1   1   1 - 2 - 3   1   1   1   1 - 2 - 3

Rhythm Writing

Use with page 19.

Circle the top number in each $\frac{4}{4}$ time signature.

The top number tells the number of beats in each measure.

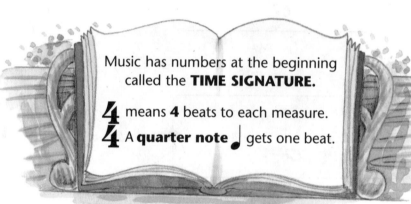

Music has numbers at the beginning called the **TIME SIGNATURE.**

$\frac{4}{4}$ means **4** beats to each measure.
A **quarter note** gets one beat.

Rhythm Reading

Play each rhythm pattern on a hand drum. Count aloud.

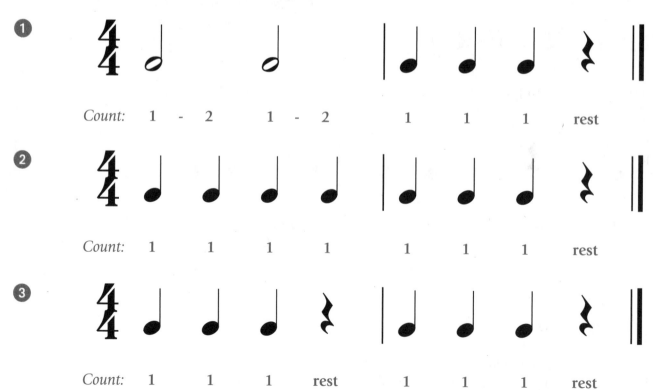

1.
Count: 1 - 2   1 - 2   1   1   1   rest

2.
Count: 1   1   1   1   1   1   1   rest

3.
Count: 1   1   1   **rest**   1   1   1   rest

Rhythm Writing

Draw a **half note** in each box.

Then, clap and count the rhythm pattern.

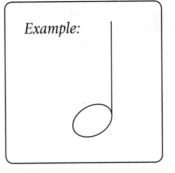
Example:

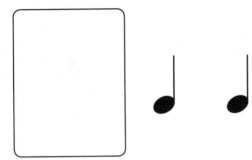 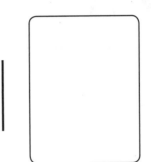 

Rhythm Reading

Tap the rhythm pattern on your lap.

Tap notes with a down stem (♩) with your LH.

Tap notes with an up stem (♩) with your RH.

Count aloud.

RH

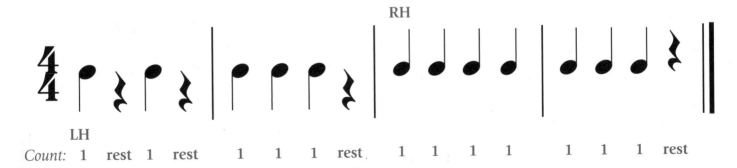

LH

Count: 1   rest   1   rest   1   1   1   rest   1   1   1   1   1   1   1   rest

Use with page 21.

Rhythm Writing

Clap the rhythm patterns. Then, draw a line to match each rhythm pattern to the music friend whose name matches the rhythm.

El-gar E. El-e-phant

Moz-art Mouse

Bee-tho-ven Bear

Rhythm Reading

1 Tap the rhythm pattern on your lap. Count aloud.

Count: 1   1   1   1   1   1   1   rest   1 - 2   1 - 2   1 - 2 - 3 - 4

2 Using finger 1 of the LH, play the above rhythm pattern on any G. Then, play again with LH finger 2.

Rhythm Writing

Draw a **quarter note** in each box.

Then, clap and count the rhythm pattern.

Example:

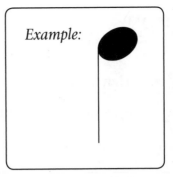

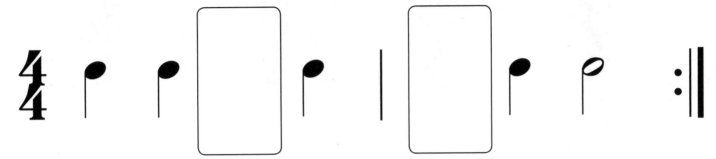

Rhythm Reading

Clap and count the rhythm patterns.

1

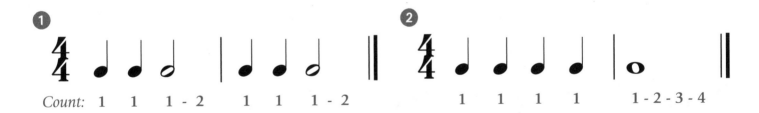

Count: 1   1   1 - 2   1   1   1 - 2   1   1   1   1   1 - 2 - 3 - 4

3

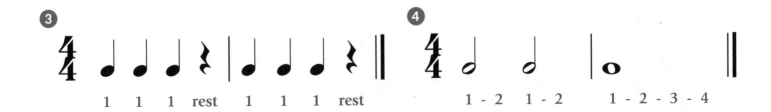

1   1   1   rest   1   1   1   rest   1 - 2   1 - 2   1 - 2 - 3 - 4

5 Play each rhythm pattern (1–4) with bells.

Rhythm Writing

Use with page 24.

Circle the top number in each **¾** time signature.

The top number tells the number of beats in each measure.

A NEW TIME SIGNATURE

¾ means **3** beats to each measure.

A **quarter note** ♩ gets one beat.

Rhythm Reading

Play each rhythm pattern on a hand drum. Count aloud.

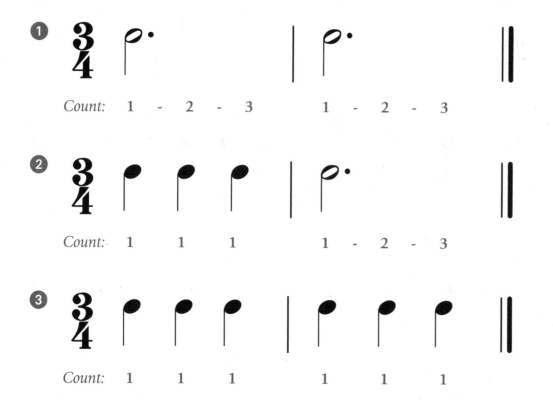

Count: 1 - 2 - 3   1 - 2 - 3

Count: 1   1   1   1 - 2 - 3

Count: 1   1   1   1   1   1

Rhythm Writing

Draw a line connecting the dots to match the rhythm patterns to their counts.

1 - 2 1 | 1 - 2 1

1 1 1 | 1 - 2 - 3

1 - 2 1 | 1 - 2 - 3

Rhythm Reading

1 Using finger 2 of the RH, play the rhythm pattern on any D. Count aloud.

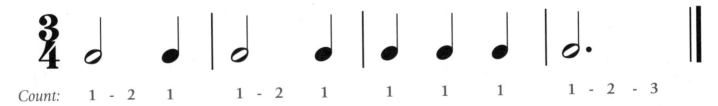

Count: 1 - 2   1   1 - 2   1   1   1   1   1 - 2 - 3

2 Using finger 2 of the LH, play the rhythm pattern on any C. Count aloud.

Count: 1   1   1   1 - 2 - 3   1 - 2   1   1 - 2 - 3

Use with page 27.

Rhythm Writing

Draw a line connecting the dots to match each rhythm pattern to its correct time signature.

Rhythm Reading

Tap the rhythm pattern on your lap. Tap notes with an up stem (♩) with your RH.

Tap notes with a down stem (♩) with your LH. Count aloud.

Count: 1 - 2   1   1 - 2   1   1   1   1   1 - 2 - 3

Rhythm Writing

1 Change each **whole note** to a **quarter note** by coloring it **black** and drawing a stem on the right.

2 Change each **half note** to a **dotted half note** by adding a dot on the right.

3 Then, clap and count the rhythm.

Rhythm Reading

Clap and count the rhythm patterns.

1

Count: 1   rest   1   rest   1   1   1   rest

2

1 - 2   1 - 2   1   1   1   rest

3

1 - 2   1   1 - 2 - 3

4

1   1   1   1 - 2 - 3

5 Play each rhythm pattern (1–4) on a wood block.

Rhythm Writing

Use with page 31.

Draw a **whole note** in each blank measure.

Then, clap and count the rhythm pattern.

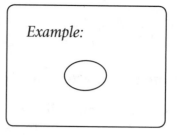

Example:

Rhythm Reading

Clap the *J. S. Bunny* rhythm pattern and chant the words.

Chant: J.   S.   Bun - ny   J.   S.   Bun - ny

Rhythm Writing

Draw a line connecting the dots to match the rhythm patterns to their counts.

𝄴 ♩ ♩ ♩ ♩ | 𝅗𝅥 𝅗𝅥 ‖ •	• **1 1 1 1** | **1 - 2 1 - 2**
𝄵 𝅗𝅥 ♩ | 𝅗𝅥. ‖ •	• **1 - 2 1 1** | **1 - 2 1 - 2**
𝄴 𝅗𝅥 ♩ ♩ | 𝅗𝅥 𝅗𝅥 ‖ •	• **1 - 2 1** | **1 - 2 - 3**

Rhythm Reading

Tap the rhythm pattern on your lap. Tap notes with a down stem (↑) with your LH.

Tap notes with an up stem (♩) with your RH. Count aloud.

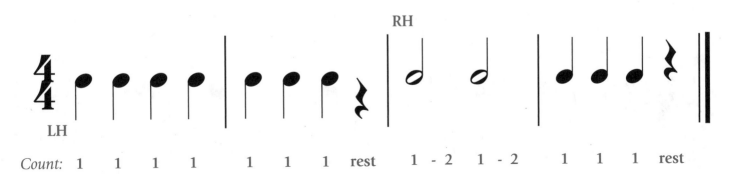

| Count: | 1 | 1 | 1 | 1 | 1 | 1 | 1 | rest | 1 - 2 | 1 - 2 | 1 | 1 | 1 | rest |

Use with page 35.

Rhythm Writing

Draw a line connecting the dots to match each rhythm pattern to its correct time signature.

Rhythm Reading

Clap and count the rhythm patterns.

1

Count: 1 - 2   1 - 2   1 - 2   1 - 2   1   1   1   1   1 - 2 - 3 - 4

2

Count: 1 - 2   1   1 - 2 - 3   1   1   1   1 - 2 - 3

Rhythm Writing

Draw two **half notes** in each blank measure.

Then, clap and count the rhythm pattern.

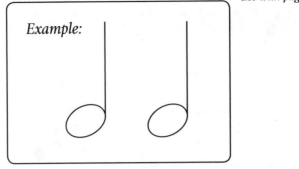

Example:

Rhythm Reading

1 Clap and count the rhythm pattern.

Count: 1 - 2   1 - 2   1 - 2   1 - 2   1   1   1   1   1   1   1   rest

2 Play the above rhythm pattern with rhythm sticks.

Use with page 39.

Rhythm Writing

Draw a line connecting the dots to match the rhythm patterns to their counts.

3/4 ♩. | ♩ ♩ ♩ | ♩. ‖ •	• 1 - 2 1 | 1 1 1 | 1 - 2 - 3
3/4 ♩ ♩ | ♩ ♩ ♩ | ♩. ‖ •	• 1 - 2 - 3 | 1 1 1 | 1 - 2 - 3
4/4 ♩ ♩ | ♩ ♩ ♩ ♩ | o ‖ •	• 1-2 1-2 | 1 1 1 1 | 1-2-3-4

Rhythm Reading

Play each rhythm pattern with rhythm sticks. Count aloud.

1

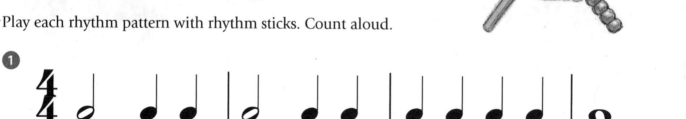

Count: 1 - 2   1   1   1 - 2   1   1   1   1   1   1   1 - 2 - 3 - 4

2

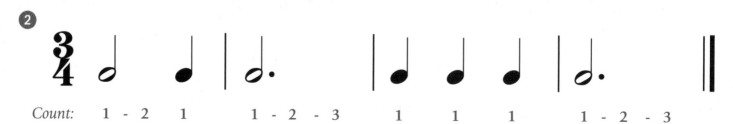

Count: 1 - 2   1   1 - 2 - 3   1   1   1   1 - 2 - 3

Rhythm Writing

Draw a line connecting the dots to match each rhythm pattern to its correct time signature.

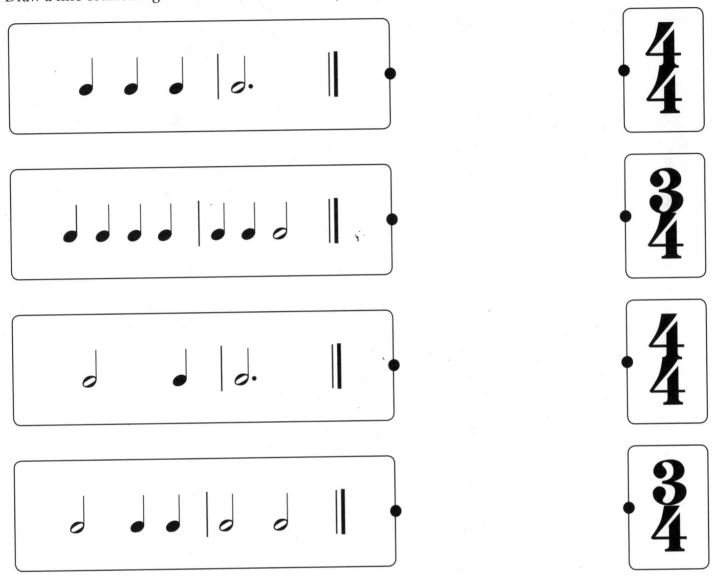

Rhythm Reading

Tap the rhythm pattern on your lap. Tap notes with an up stem (♩) with your RH.

Tap notes with a down stem (⌐) with your LH. Count aloud.

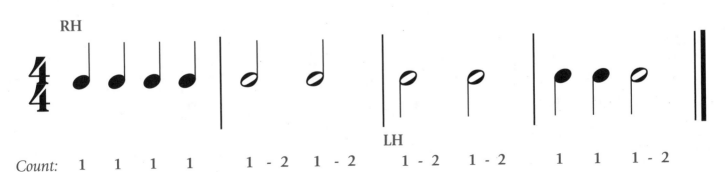

Count: 1   1   1   1   1 - 2 1 - 2   1 - 2 1 - 2   1   1   1 - 2

Rhythm Writing

Use with page 43.

Draw a **dotted half note** in each blank measure.

Then, clap and count the rhythm pattern.

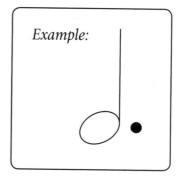
Example:

Rhythm Reading

Clap and count the rhythm patterns.

 1

Count: 1 - 2   1   1   1   1

2

1   1   1   1 - 2 - 3

3

1   1   1 - 2   1   1   1 - 2

4

1 - 2   1 - 2   1 - 2 - 3 - 4

5 Play each rhythm pattern (1–4) with rhythm sticks.

Rhythm Writing

Draw a line connecting the dots to match the rhythm patterns to their counts.

1 1 1 1 | 1 - 2 - 3 - 4

1 1 1 - 2 | 1 1 1 - 2

1 - 2 1 | 1 - 2 1

Rhythm Reading

1 Using finger 3 of the RH, play the rhythm pattern on any F. Count aloud.

Count: 1 - 2 1 - 2   1 - 2 rest -2   1   1   1   1   1 - 2 rest -2

2 Using finger 3 of the LH, play the rhythm pattern on any E. Count aloud.

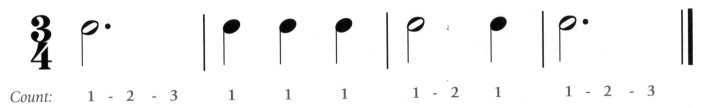

Count: 1 - 2 - 3   1   1   1   1 - 2 1   1 - 2 - 3

Use with page 47.

Rhythm Writing

Draw a line connecting the dots to match each rhythm pattern to its correct time signature.

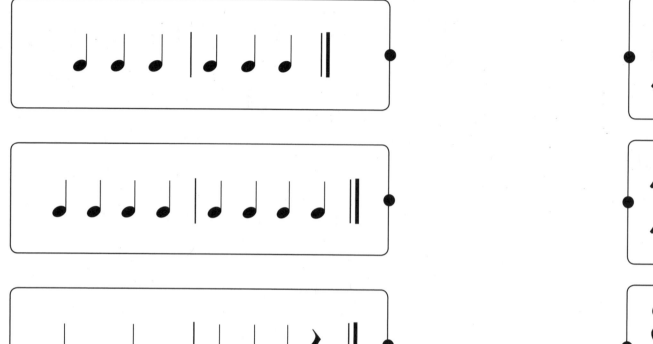

Rhythm Reading

Clap the *Pachelbel Penguin* rhythm pattern and chant the words.

Chant: **Pach - el - bel   Pen - guin   (rest)**